MONSTROUS MYTHS

Terrible Tales of
ANCIENT EGYPT

Clare Hibbert

FRANKLIN WATTS
LONDON • SYDNEY

First published in 2014 by Franklin Watts

Copyright © 2014 Arcturus Publishing Limited

Franklin Watts
338 Euston Road
London NW1 3BH

Franklin Watts Australia
Level 17/207 Kent Street, Sydney NSW 2000

Produced by Arcturus Publishing Limited,
26/27 Bickels Yard, 151–153 Bermondsey Street, London SE1 3HA

Illustrations: Janos Jantner (Beehive Illustration)
Editor: Joe Harris
Designer: Emma Randall
Cover designer: Emma Randall

A CIP catalogue record for this book is available from the British Library.

Dewey Decimal Classification Number 398.2'0932
ISBN 978 1 4451 2941 9

Printed in China

Franklin Watts is a division of Hachette Children's Books, an Hachette
UK company.

www.hachette.co.uk

SL003832EN
Supplier 03, Date 0114, Print Run 3027

CONTENTS

Ancient Egyptian Stories...4

Savage Sekhmet's Rampage..6

Set's Deadly Banquet 10

Horus Has His Revenge 14

The Treasure Thief 18

Visit to the Land of the Dead 22

The Sailor and the Snake..26

Glossary 30

Further Reading and Websites 31

Index 32

ANCIENT EGYPTIAN STORIES

Travel back in time more than 5,000 years to the banks of the Nile river in northeast Africa. Here you'll find one of the earliest civilizations – ancient Egypt.

The Egyptians were real clever clogs. Their engineers built jaw-dropping buildings – the pyramids, of course, and palaces and temples, too – and their scribes wrote down all sorts of stuff, from shopping receipts to laws and stories. Being so good at everything, it's not surprising that the Egyptians' civilization lasted about 3,000 years.

The Egyptians believed that the sun god Ra carried the sun across the sky in his boat every day.

The people of ancient Egypt worshipped hundreds of gods and goddesses and had stories about how those deities came to be. One myth told how the sun god Ra created the first people and the first gods. The Egyptians believed that their rulers, the pharaohs, were gods descended from Ra. At times they even thought that the pharaoh *was* the sun god, come to Earth.

Ra sometimes looked all-human but more often he was shown with a falcon's head on a man's body. Sounds mixed up? That was the norm for Egyptian gods and goddesses. The protector goddess Bastet had the head of a cat while Anubis, god of the dead, had a jackal's head. Anubis was one of the most important gods because he protected the dead on their journey into the afterlife.

The Egyptians put a lot of effort into preparing for the afterlife. They thought they would still need their bodies, so they were preserved as mummies. Embalmers sometimes wore jackal masks to look like Anubis!

Believe it or not!

Egyptian stories were written down in picture writing (hieroglyphs) on papyrus scrolls. Some scrolls have survived to this day, though they're looking a bit tatty around the edges now!

SAVAGE SEKHMET'S RAMPAGE

Ra's daughter could switch between harmless Hathor and deadly, lion-headed Sekhmet.

Ra was a very powerful god and the first-ever pharaoh. He was so mighty that he'd created the earth and the sky, the winds and the rain. Even his snot was amazing – he managed to sneeze out a couple of gods. Achoo!

Ra's reign, which lasted thousands of years, was a time of peace and plenty. Eventually, though, he grew old and the people started grumbling among themselves. Some even began to worship Ra's arch enemy, the evil serpent Apep. Talk about exact opposites! Ra soared; Apep slithered. Ra brought light; Apep was god of night and darkness. Ra brought order to the world; Apep brought chaos.

Ra saw that the people were getting a bit rebellious – and he didn't like it one bit. So he called a meeting of his top gods and goddesses and told them his plan. He reckoned that the only way to show the humans who was boss was to destroy the lot of them. He called on his daughter Hathor to help. It was hard to see how Hathor, a goddess of love, could wreak revenge on anyone – but then she transformed into her lioness form, Sekhmet!

Super-destructive Sekhmet set to work. Although she was huge, she was speedy and she made short work of running down her prey. By the end of the first day, Upper Egypt looked like the set of a horror movie.

When it came to death and destruction, Sekhmet always got the lion's share!

NILE EVENING NEWS

Lethal Lion-Lady on the Loose!

Readers are advised to stay indoors until further notice. The goddess Sekhmet has gone berserk, and has been eating anything that moves... and many things that don't. The exact death toll has yet to be confirmed, as our entire team of reporters has been devoured. However, as the sun sets over the desert this evening, Sekhmet is sleeping off her monstrous meal. Will she strike again tomorrow?

The few survivors prayed desperately to Ra, and he took pity on them. After all, what was the point of ruling a land that had no people left? But now Sekhmet had tasted blood, she'd be hard to stop. Ra needed a plan.

Ra set all his priestesses and serving girls to work crushing barley for beer. In all, they brewed 7,000 jars of the stuff and then mixed it with red ochre to look like blood. Ra tipped out the jars where Sekhmet was sleeping – and waited.

When the goddess woke up, all set to begin another killing spree, she saw the 'blood'-covered fields. Thinking the blood was left over from her victims, Sekhmet laughed, licked her lips and began to drink. She didn't stop until she had drunk the whole lot! Feeling woozy, she returned to her father Ra, who transformed her back into gentle Hathor. Phew!

Believe it or not!

Beer in ancient Egypt wasn't strongly alcoholic like today's beer. Everyone drank it — even kids! In some ways, it was more like a sloppy meal than a drink — thick and rather porridgy. Yuck!

Kindly Hathor was a popular goddess. You wouldn't want to get on her bad side, though!

SET'S DEADLY BANQUET

Most brothers and sisters squabble sometimes. They might even have the odd fight. But trapping your brother in a box and chucking him into a fast-flowing river... that's taking sibling rivalry a bit far!

Osiris and Set were brothers. Their parents were Nut, the sky goddess, and Geb, the god of the earth – the first two gods that mighty Ra had created. When Ra finally stopped being pharaoh, he chose Osiris to succeed him. Osiris' sister-wife Isis became queen. And that made Set very jealous... jealous enough to commit murder.

Set built a beautiful wooden chest as a trap for Osiris.

Set was cunning. He hosted a magnificent banquet in Osiris' honour. The other guests were wicked conspirators, loyal to Set. At the end of the meal, Set unveiled a fabulous chest made of rare and costly woods – cedar from Lebanon and ebony from Ethiopia. Set announced that he'd give the chest to the guest who fitted into it most perfectly.

Talk about bling! The dazzling chest was decorated with gold, silver, ivory, lapis lazuli and precious stones.

One by one, the guests climbed into the chest. All were too fat or too thin, too tall or too short. But when it came to Osiris' turn, his body was a perfect fit. It was no accident. Sneaky Set had built the chest to his brother's exact body measurements!

Osiris' delight that he fitted the chest didn't last long. 'Yes, you fit it! And you can keep it, alright – as your coffin!' gloated Set. With that, he slammed down the lid, nailed it shut and threw the chest into the Nile.

When Osiris' wife, Isis, found out what had happened to her husband, she was distraught. Even though she was heavily pregnant, she set out to look for the chest. She took a break to give birth to her son, Horus, then left the baby and continued her search.

Isis learned that the chest had come ashore at Byblos, in modern-day Lebanon. A tree had grown around it and now it was a pillar in the royal palace. Isis disguised herself so that she could take a job there, as nanny to the king and queen's sickly son. With her help, the prince quickly grew stronger.

Isis' nephew, Anubis, used his dog-like senses to help her search for her husband.

The queen heard strange stories about her new nanny. She decided to hide herself and spy on Isis and the little prince. She watched as Isis built up a huge fire. Then, suddenly, Isis flung the boy into the flames. She turned into a bird and began to fly around Osiris' pillar, squawking. The horrified queen leaped from her hiding place to snatch her son from the fire.

Isis changed back into her normal form. It was time for some explanation! She had taken a shine to the prince, and had been burning away his human self so he could become a god. Thanks to the queen's meddling, he would have to stay mortal. Then Isis told the queen about Osiris' body being trapped in the pillar.

The pillar was split open, and Isis returned to Egypt with her husband's coffin. But it wasn't a happy ending. Wicked Set discovered the coffin, pulled out Osiris' body and chopped it into 14 pieces, scattering them all over Egypt. Isis had to go out looking for him... all over again. Anubis, the god of the mummification, agreed to help her in her quest.

Believe it or not!
In one version of this story, the Nile was said to have flowed from Isis' tears, as she wept for her dead husband.

HORUS HAS HIS REVENGE

As unhappy childhoods go, Horus' was right up there. His dad, Osiris, was murdered before he was even born. Then his mum, Isis, abandoned him when he was a brand-new baby, to go looking for his dad's body.

Horus spent his early years hiding from his dad's killer, his wicked uncle Set. One day, Set found Horus' hideout. He turned himself into a scorpion, sneaked into the lad's cradle and stung him. The sting seemed to drain all the life out of Horus! Horrified, Isis rushed to ask for advice from Thoth, the god of knowledge.

Horus had every right to be the next pharaoh when he grew up. After all, he was Osiris' son!

14

Thoth told Isis that the child would recover. What a relief! He also called a council of the gods to settle who should be pharaoh: Set, who had seized the throne from his brother, Osiris, or little Horus. Set said he'd start a war if anyone tried to take power from him. But plenty of gods thought it was wrong for Set, a murderer, to be ruler.

Set had banned Isis from the council, but she sneaked in, wearing a cunning disguise. She had made herself look like Set's ex-wife, Nephthys, who'd left in disgust when Set killed Osiris. Set was so glad his wife had come back that he couldn't think straight. Isis easily got him to swear that her son would be pharaoh. When Set realised he'd been tricked, he was furious.

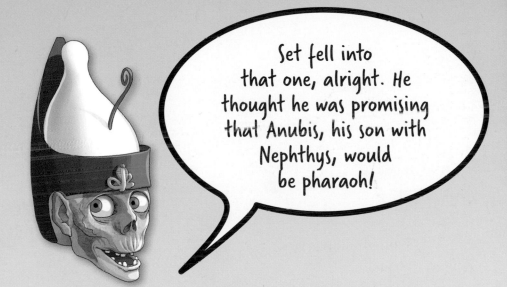

Set fell into that one, alright. He thought he was promising that Anubis, his son with Nephthys, would be pharaoh!

Young Horus recovered from the scorpion's sting just as Thoth had said that he would. Over the next few years, he trained for battle. He had to be ready to take on his uncle!

When Set discovered that Horus was preparing to fight, he decided to attack him straight away. But ancient Egyptian gods didn't just go in for punching and kicking. They preferred to fight tooth and claw – literally – by transforming into animals!

Set fought his last battle as a monstrous red hippo. Ever after, the Egyptians believed that male hippos were evil.

The Big Fight

It's the grudge-match of the century, as Horus, the bird-headed bruiser, takes on Set, the undefeated champion! Set charges Horus in the form of a big, black boar, hurling blinding light into his eyes. Horus can't see a thing. It's Round One to Set!

But what's this? Horus has used a spell to make Set's loyal soldiers attack each other. Set's men have transformed themselves into crocodiles and hippos... but Horus has used chains to tangle them up! And now Horus is getting more hands-on – or talons-on, we should say. He's changed into a hawk and torn them to pieces!

Set's back in the fight, and he's wearing the half-rotten head of some dead beast. Stinky! It looks like Horus is going to smash him in the face with a mace... and yes, it's all over for Set!

Horus took Set to the council of the gods. The supreme god, Ra, decreed that Horus could hack Set to pieces just as Set had chopped up his dad! But Set had one last trick: his spirit slipped out of his body, and entered a snake. He slithered south to gather new followers.

In their final battle, Set turned into a huge hippo. Just as he was about to swallow up his nephew's boat, Horus' harpoon struck home. Set the hippo sank, dead, to the bottom of the Nile. At last Horus could rule in peace without any more 'beastly' fighting!

Believe it or not!

For the Egyptians, Horus was the god of the sky, war, hunting and protection.

THE TREASURE THIEF

You've probably heard of life insurance. But have you head of *afterlife* insurance? Rich Egyptians built their tombs while they were still alive. When they died, they were buried with plenty of treasure, to make them wealthy in the next life.

Where did all the treasure come from? Pharaohs and nobles spent years saving it up in treasure houses. So of course treasure houses were a favourite target for greedy robbers! And not all thieves were rough-and-ready rogues. Take Horemheb, for example...

Ramses III realized his treasure was going missing, so he set spiky traps to catch the thieves.

Horemheb was an architect. When Rameses III asked him to build his treasure house, he sneakily added a secret passageway so he could cream off some of the pharaoh's treasure. Horemheb died soon after – but not before passing on his secret to his sons.

What a 'golden' opportunity for Horemheb's sons!

When the pharaoh noticed his gold and jewels were being snaffled, he set traps. And before long, one of the brothers got spiked. 'Chop off my head, brother!' he pleaded. 'I don't want a slow and painful death. The pharaoh might torture me. Take my head so there are no clues to lead to our family. Save yourself and look after poor old Mum.' Gritting his teeth, the second man put his brother out of his misery.

The pharaoh was not at all pleased to find a horrible, headless torso in his trap. Determined to catch the one that got away, he hung up the body outside the palace. Sure enough, the dead man's mum rose to the bait. 'Please – pretty please! Steal his body back!' she begged her second son.

Of course, the pharaoh had stationed guards near the headless body. The cunning treasure thief disguised himself as an old merchant and staged a little drama for the guards. He 'accidentally' leaked some wineskins right by them. When they leaped up to help, he rewarded them with plenty more wine. Soon the guards were snoring loudly and the treasure thief could steal away with his brother's body.

Outfoxed again, the pharaoh tried another trap. He disguised one of his daughters as a visiting noblewoman and spread a rumour that she'd marry the man who'd done the cleverest, wickedest thing.

The treasure thief played an 'armless' trick on the pharaoh's daughter!

The treasure thief saw through the set-up at once, but couldn't resist outwitting the pharaoh again. He went to the princess's tent and told her how he'd stolen from the pharaoh, sliced off his own brother's head and tricked the drunken guards.

What he didn't tell her was that he'd hidden the arm of a dead man under his cloak! As he finished his tale, the princess grabbed what she thought was his arm and called out to her guards. However, the guards found her clutching a lifeless arm – and the treasure thief had snuck away.

The pharaoh had to hand it to the treasure thief. He truly was clever! Preferring to have him as a friend not a foe, the pharaoh pardoned him and let him marry his daughter. He also made the thief so rich that he never needed to steal ever again. What a forgiving fellow!

Believe it or not!

Although Rameses III was a real pharaoh, there were many myths about him. One told how he met and fell in love with Helen of Troy.

VISIT TO THE LAND OF THE DEAD

Imagine having a free pass to visit the Land of the Dead – and return safely! For the amazing Se-Osiris and his dad, all it took was a bit of magic.

Se-Osiris was a brilliantly gifted boy magician. His beginnings weren't exactly humble. His dad, Setna, was Egypt's crown prince, and his grandfather was just about the most famous pharaoh of all time, Rameses the Great.

One day, Setna and Se-Osiris saw two funeral processions pass the palace. One was a rich man's funeral. Priests headed the procession and the mummy was in a case decorated with gold. The throng of servants and mourners were weighed down with gifts to place in the man's tomb. The second was a labourer's funeral. His two sons carried his body in a simple box. The only mourners were the man's widow and his daughters-in-law.

> Se-Osiris was a boy wonder. At 12 he was already being called the greatest magician that Egypt had ever known!

As far as Setna was concerned, it was a no-brainer deciding which funeral he'd rather have. He wasn't too pleased when Se-Osiris said he hoped he'd have the poor man's funeral. 'Listen! Before you get in a huge huff, let me take you somewhere,' Se-Osiris said.

They went to the nearby Temple of Osiris, where the child magician drew magic circles, chucked around some magic powder and cast some spells. The next thing Setna knew, he was looking down at his own lifeless body! Se-Osiris had released their souls in the form of golden birds. Now they could fly to the Land of the Dead.

Flying through the air with his son's spirit was already pretty weird for Setna, but he was going to see some even stranger sights. The pair followed Ra's golden boat, which was carrying the souls of the dead along a ghostly river to the Land of the Dead.

The Land of the Dead was not a good place for anyone suffering from a fear of snakes! Half a dozen massive serpents lay curled up by the river and there were also 'guard snakes' that breathed fire like dragons.

Nothing in the Land of the Dead was more terrifying than the goddess Ammit, the Devourer of Souls. She was part-crocodile, part-lion and part-hippo.

The souls got off Ra's golden boat at Osiris' Hall of Judgement. The ibis-headed god of wisdom, Thoth, led each soul before Osiris and Anubis. Osiris, god of the afterlife, listened to each soul as they told him whether they deserved a good or bad fate. Anubis, protector of the dead, stood with his scales, to weigh their hearts.

A TRAVELLER'S GUIDE TO THE AFTERLIFE
by Crown Prince Setna

There are two possible destinations for souls leaving the Hall of Judgement: either they travel on to the fabulous Fields of Peace (a real five-star resort), or they end up in Ammit's hungry mouth.

When Anubis weighed a poor labourer's heart, he saw that the labourer had spoken the truth to Osiris, so he was sent to the Fields of Peace. But the rich man who was next in line had lied. He was tossed to the monstrous Ammit, who wolfed down his heart, then chucked his empty soul into her Pit of Fire!

After witnessing that, we flew back home. What a relief it was to be back in the Land of the Living!

Believe it or not!
Many Egyptians were buried with a copy of the Book of the Dead. It was a guidebook for passing through the Land of the Dead to the afterlife!

THE SAILOR AND THE SNAKE

As adventure stories go, it's hard to beat a shipwreck. Add in a monster and some treasure and you've got all the ingredients for a top tale – who cares if no one knows the name of the main character?!

The sailor was washed up on the beach of a mysterious island.

Not a story about shipwrecks! They always give me a sinking feeling...

One of the Egyptians' favourite stories was about a sailor onboard a boat heading to the pharaoh's mines. The ship, crewed by 150 rowers, hit trouble out at sea – a massive storm! It didn't stand a chance against the high winds and towering waves. After being blown seriously off course, the boat was dashed against some rocks and sank. Everyone drowned except that one sailor.

Clinging to a piece of floating wood, the sailor made it to a nearby island. After the horrors of the storm, this felt like paradise! The weather was hot and sunny, but there were lots of trees to provide shade. Best of all, there was more food than he could eat in a lifetime – juicy melons, figs and berries, delicious herbs and plenty of slow-moving fish and birds to catch and eat, too!

By day three, the sailor was feeling strong enough to dig a fire pit. First he made an offering to the gods to thank them for saving his life, and then he cooked himself a feast fit for a king. Afterwards he stretched out feeling very content until...

Smash! Bash! Crash! His doze was interrupted by a thundering noise. It was the sound of a giant serpent thrashing through the undergrowth straight towards him, knocking down trees with its huge tail. Uh oh! Was the sailor about to become a snake snack?

The serpent wasn't just massive – he could also speak, and breathe fire! He said that he would burn the sailor to a crisp unless he told him his story. Then he picked him up and carried him back to his lair. Trembling, the poor sailor explained that he'd been shipwrecked.

Despite his scary appearance, the snake was really rather kind. He comforted the sailor and said that he knew for sure a ship would come to rescue him in four months' time. Then he shared his own sad story. Once, he said, the island had been home to 75 snakes and he had been their king. But one day a meteorite fell from the sky and struck the snake village. All the others were killed, including his precious daughter, and now he had to live on the island all alone.

The giant snake carried the terrified sailor all the way to his cave.

The sailor promised to tell the pharaoh about the island and to send oils, perfumes and treasures to the snake. But the snake just laughed. He had all he needed, he said. And anyway, his island was magic and would vanish when the sailor left.

When the four months were up, an Egyptian ship appeared on the horizon. The serpent king gave the sailor parting gifts to pass on to the pharaoh – baboons, ivory, spices and precious perfumes. As the sailor sailed away, he looked back. Just as the snake had said, the island had completely disappeared. Crazy!

Believe it or not!

The ancient Egyptians built their seagoing boats from cedar wood, which they bought from Phoenician traders from present-day Lebanon.

GLOSSARY

afterlife Life after death.

conspirator Someone who plots with others to bring about harm.

embalmer Someone who preserves bodies so they won't decay.

fire pit A hollow in the ground where a fire could be lit for cooking and warmth.

harpoon A spear-like weapon attached to a long rope, used for catching fish and other water creatures.

hieroglyphs Picture writing.

ibis A long-billed, long-legged wading bird. The Egyptians held the ibis to be sacred as a symbol of their god of wisdom, Thoth.

jackal A wild dog that hunts or scavenges in packs, and that lives in Africa and southern Asia. The Egyptians held the jackal to be sacred as a symbol of their god of the dead, Anubis.

lapis lazuli A semi-precious, bright-blue stone.

mace A metal club with a spiked head.

meteorite A shooting star, or piece of space rock, that falls to Earth.

mortal A being that will die. Ordinary human beings are mortal, whereas gods are immortal (they won't die).

mummy An embalmed body.

ochre An earthy red pigment.

papyrus A reed that grows near the Nile. The Egyptians used strips of papyrus stems to make a kind of paper.

pharaoh A ruler of ancient Egypt.

pyramid A monument that is square at the bottom and pointed at the top, built by the Egyptians as a royal tomb.

scribe Someone who wrote letters and other documents for a living.

scroll An ancient book made from a long roll of papyrus, paper or parchment.

sister-wife Someone who is both a sister and a wife. In the ancient Egyptian royal family it was usual for brothers and sisters to marry and rule together as pharaoh and queen.

succeed To take over a title or position from someone.

Upper Egypt The southern region of ancient Egypt, whose main city was Thebes. The northern region, Lower Egypt, was where the Nile emptied into the Mediterranean. Its main city was Memphis.

wineskin An animal skin sewn up to make a bag to contain wine.

FURTHER INFORMATION

Further Reading

The Awesome Egyptians by Terry Deary (Scholastic, 2007)

Egyptian Myths by Kathy Elgin and Fiona Sansom (Franklin Watts, 2012)

Egyptian Myths and Legends by Fiona Macdonald (Raintree, 2013)

Graphic Myths: Egyptian Myths by Gary Jeffrey (Book House, 2007)

Stories from Ancient Egypt by Joyce Tyldesley (Oxbow Books, 2012)

The War of Horus and Set by David A McIntee (Osprey Publishing, 2013)

Websites

egypt.mrdonn.org/gods
A website about Egyptian gods and goddesses aimed specifically at kids.

www.ancientegypt.co.uk
An exploration of ancient Egypt using objects from the British Museum's collection.

www.bbc.co.uk/history/ancient/egyptians
The BBC's guide to ancient Egypt, with sections on gods and beliefs and hieroglyphs.

www.ducksters.com/history/ancient_egypt
Lots of information about different aspects of ancient Egyptian life.

www.egyptianmyths.net
A website with information about ancient Egyptian mythology and religion.

INDEX

afterlife 5, 18, 25
Ammit 24, 25
animals 5, 6, 12, 13, 14, 16–17, 24, 27–29
Anubis 5, 12, 25
Apep 6–7

Bastet 5
Book of the Dead 25

embalmers 5

Geb 10
gods 5, 7
  council of 15, 17
  of the dead/afterlife 5, 25
  of the Earth 10
  of knowledge 14
  of mummification 13
  of night and darkness 6
  of the sky 17
  of the sun 4, 5

of war, hunting and protection 17
goddesses 5, 7
  of love 7
  protector 5
  of the sky 10

Hathor 6, 7, 9
Helen of Troy 21
hieroglyphs 5
Horemheb 18, 19
Horus 12, 14–17

Isis 10–13, 14–15

Land of the Dead 22-25

mummies 5, 22

Nephthys 8, 15
Nile 4, 11, 13, 17
Nut 10

Osiris 10–13, 14, 15, 23, 25

pharaohs 5, 6, 10, 14, 15, 18–21, 27, 29
pyramids 4

Ra 4, 5, 6–9, 17, 24, 25
Ramses III 18, 19, 21
Ramses the Great 22

Se-Osiris 22–25
Sekhmet 6–9
Set 10–13, 14–17
Setna 22–25

Thoth 14–15, 25

SERIES CONTENTS

Terrible Tales of Africa

African Stories · Anansi the Spiderman · Horrible Little Hlakanyana · The Big, Bad Bird · The Cave of Bones · The Crafty Jackal · The Seven-Headed Serpent

Terrible Tales of Ancient Egypt

Ancient Egyptian Stories · Savage Sekhmet's Rampage · Set's Deadly Banquet · Horus Has His Revenge · The Treasure Thief · Visit to the Land of the Dead · The Sailor and the Snake

Terrible Tales of Ancient Greece

Greek Stories and Legends · Heracles the Hero · Perseus and the Snake-Haired Horror · Hunt for the Golden Fleece · Locking Horns with the Minotaur · How a Horse Ended a War · The Longest Journey Home — Ever!

Terrible Tales of Ancient Rome

Roman Stories and Legends · Aeneas the Adventurer · Journey to the Underworld · Brotherly Love — Or Not! · The Jealous Goddess · Life in the Land of the Dead · Cupid's Revenge

Terrible Tales of the Middle Ages

Medieval Stories · George and the Dragon · The Legendary King · The Green Knight · Quest for the Grail · Beowulf · Outside the Law

Terrible Tales of Native America

Native American Stories · Glooscap and the Water Monster · The Great Thunderbird · The Menace of Man-Eagle · Coyote's Sticky Situation · Coyote Inside the Giant · Wildcat and Great Rabbit · The Maiden's Revenge